Stay Engaged

Practicing Empathy

Reach Out!

Learning to overcome negative thoughts and stay mindful is not the same as fighting depression. Do you feel overwhelmed by sadness? Remember, you matter. You are not alone. If you need help, reach out. Talk to an adult you love and trust. This could be a teacher, school counselor, or family member. Make an appointment with your doctor. Seek professional help. Or call the National Suicide Prevention Lifeline at 1-800-273-8255. Someone is available to talk with you 24 hours a day, every day.

45TH PARALLEL PRESS

Published in the United States of America by Cherry Lake Publishing
Ann Arbor, Michigan
www.cherrylakepublishing.com

Reading Adviser: Marla Conn, MS, Ed., Literacy specialist, Read-Ability, Inc.
Book Designer: Melinda Millward

Photo Credits: © Antonio Guillem/Shutterstock.com, back cover, 8; © monkeybusinessimages/istockphoto.com, cover, 5; © Sudowoodo/Shutterstock.com, 6; © Norb_KM/Shutterstock.com, 7; © Olkita/Shutterstock.com, 10; © Stasia04/Shutterstock.com, 11; © Shooting Star Studio/Shutterstock.com, 12; © davooda/Shutterstock.com, 14; © kali9/istockphoto.com, 15; © JohnnyGreig/istockphoto.com, 16; © fstop123/istockphoto.com, 17; © kuroksta/Shutterstock.com, 18; © Monkey Business Images/Shutterstock.com, 19; © popicon/Shutterstock.com, 20; © Puckung/Shutterstock.com, 22, 26; © Nattakorn_Maneerat/Shutterstock.com, 23; © exopixel/Shutterstock.com, 24; © Rawpixel.com/Shutterstock.com, 25; © RimDream/Shutterstock.com, 27; © vdimage/Shutterstock.com, 28; © Dmytro Zinkevych/Shutterstock.com, 30

GGraphic Element Credits: © kkoman/Shutterstock.com, back cover, front cover, multiple interior pages; © str33t cat/Shutterstock.com, front cover, multiple interior pages; © NotionPic/Shutterstock.com, multiple interior pages; © CARACOLLA/Shutterstock.com, multiple interior pages; © VikiVector/Shutterstock.com, multiple interior pages

45th Parallel Press is an imprint of Cherry Lake Publishing.

Library of Congress Cataloging-in-Publication Data has been filed and is available at catalog.loc.gov

Printed in the United States of America
Corporate Graphics

Table of Contents

INTRODUCTION

Have you ever felt sorry for someone? Have you ever cried because you saw another person cry?

People have **emotions**. Emotions are feelings. People get hurt. They feel pain. They need support. They need people who can understand them.

Empathy means you can feel another person's emotions. It means you understand where a person is coming from. It means you can see things from different sides.

This book gives you tips on how to be **mindful**. Mindful means being aware. It means taking care of your body and mind. Take a moment. Practice having empathy. Just breathe …

Tip: Choose to show empathy. Do this by sharing in the other person's feelings.

CHAPTER ONE
Listen Actively

To have empathy, you must listen. Being a good listener is an important skill. Active listening is not easy to do. Pay attention. Be fully present. Focus on the moment. Try not to be distracted. Listen.

Check your **biases**. A bias is favoring an idea over another based on feelings. When people are biased, they might not give another idea an equal chance. Ask yourself:

- Do I have an open mind? Or have I already made up my mind?
- Am I ready to listen to the whole story?
- Do I really want to understand? Or do I just want to share what I think?

Tip: Talk to a friend. Practice active listening. Ask questions. Summarize your talk.

First, listen and connect.

- Make eye contact and sit close.
- Let people talk. Don't **interrupt**. Interrupt means to cut in before it's your turn.

Second, listen and reflect.

- Repeat what the speaker is saying. Say, "What I'm hearing is …"

Third, listen and **affirm**. Affirm means to support.

- Let the speaker know you're listening. Nod your head.
- Honor the speaker's feelings. Ask, "Are you feeling …"

Fourth, listen and encourage.

- Ask questions.
- Thank the speaker for sharing.

Tip: Know that people always change. Don't hold on to **grudges**.

Real-Life Scenarios

Life is full of adventures. There will be challenges. Things happen. Make good choices. These are some events you could face:

- Your best friend's parents are getting a divorce. Your best friend is really sad. She's crying. How does this make you feel? How can you connect to your friend? How can you be a better listener?
- You are playing a sports game. People are picking teams. You see a classmate get picked last. How do you think this person feels? What can you do to make the person feel better?
- You see a new kid at school. How would you feel if you were the new kid? What would you do? How can you make the new kid feel more welcome?

CHAPTER TWO
See Another Side

Empathy means being able to see different **points of view**. Points of view are ways of seeing. Each person sees the same thing differently. It's important to be mindful of different views. Put yourself in another person's place. Feel what they're feeling. See how they see things. You don't have to agree. But you have to understand that not everyone sees things the way you do.

Practice learning about different points of view. Do this by reading a book. Or watch a movie.

- Identify the main character. Recall the story from the main character's viewpoint.
- Pick another character. Tell the story from that character's viewpoint. What changed? How did you see things differently?

Tip: Imagine the main character of a well-known book or movie as a different gender or race. How would the story change?

Practice with a new friend. Take this opportunity to get to know someone better.

- Introduce yourself. Make **small talk**. Small talk is talking about unimportant things. It helps set up deeper talks. An example topic is weather.
- Tell a story about your life. For example, talk about getting your first pet.
- Have your friend retell your story. Have your friend tell it from their viewpoint. Have your friend share feelings and thoughts.
- Switch. Listen to your friend's story. Retell your friend's story from your viewpoint.
- Talk about how you saw the same events. What did you have in common? What was different?

Tip: Think of a time when someone was mean to you. Put yourself in that person's place. See the situation from that person's point of view.

Science Connection

Some people have too much empathy. They care too much. They have "hyper-empathy syndrome." A syndrome is a condition connected to a group of symptoms. People with hyper-empathy syndrome pick up every emotion around them. They lose themselves in other people's needs. They spend more time caring about others than themselves. They feel guilty for other people's pain. They get sick when others are unhappy. They don't know how to control their emotions. They can't stop crying. They get really mad. Having too much empathy is dangerous. It causes a lot of stress. It can make people tired. It leads to burnout. Burnout is when a person becomes exhausted or worn out. They can't handle their lives anymore. They can no longer function. That's why mindfulness is so important. We need to take care of ourselves. That way, we can take care of others better.

CHAPTER THREE
Look for Connections

Having empathy means feeling connected. Practice making connections. But this can be hard. Instead of focusing on differences, focus on how we're the same. Focus on what we have in common. All humans need food, water, and **shelter**. Shelters are homes. All humans need love.

Be mindful when you meet people. Keep an open mind. Say these things in your head:

- Just like me, this person wants to be happy.
- Just like me, this person wants to avoid pain.
- Just like me, this person has been sad.
- Just like me, this person has needs.
- Just like me, this person is learning to live a good life.

Tip: Think about something or someone you love. Imagine sending love and compassion. Focus on the warm feelings.

There will be times when you meet new people. Take time to get to know each other. Take time to introduce yourselves. Take time to see what you have in common.

Try playing the "I Am" game.

- Stand in a circle.
- Have a person stand in the middle. Have that person share a truth or fact about themselves. An example is "I am left-handed."
- Have people from the circle step into the middle if they share the same truth or fact.
- Have the person in the middle choose a new person. Play again.

Tip: Start saying "we" or "us." Say "I" or "me" less often. Change your language.

CHAPTER FOUR
Act It Out

There's so much going on in the world today. The news is full of good and bad stories. Talking about **current** events is important. Current means happening right now. We need to be aware of what's happening. We also need to talk about our thoughts and feelings about these events. Think about a current event. Ask yourself:

- How might the people involved be feeling?
- How would I feel in their shoes?
- What can I do to help?

Then, act out the current event. Write a short play. Play the parts. Practice seeing the event from different points of view.

Tip: Watch several movies about the same event. Think about what you learned. What were the similarities and differences?

Role-playing is a great way to practice empathy. Role-playing is acting out the part of a character. You have to pretend to be someone you're not. You have to change your behavior. You have to get into your character.

- Think about different situations. For example, think about a situation where a friend has hurt feelings.
- Play 2 roles. One role is the person needing support. The other role is the person with empathy.
- Think about how your character would respond to the situation. Use your own experiences to help you feel connected to the role. Recall moments when you felt the same emotions.
- Return to your real self. Think about what you would do in real life.

Tip: Make a chart of emojis. Include different emotions. Act out each emoji.

Spotlight Biography

Harriet Beecher Stowe lived from 1811 to 1896. She was an American writer. She's famous for writing *Uncle Tom's Cabin*. She published this in 1852. She wrote about how bad slavery was. She didn't like how slaves were treated on southern plantations. Plantations are large houses and farms. Stowe's book sold 4 million copies in its first 10 years. It changed how people thought about slavery. Stowe felt empathy for the slaves. She was inspired to write the book after her son died. Her son died at 18 months old. He died of a sickness. His death caused Stowe great sadness. She felt bad for African American slave women whose children were taken away from them. She said, "It was at (my son's) bed, and at his grave, that I learnt what a poor slave mother may feel when her child is torn away from her."

CHAPTER FIVE
Be Kind

Be mindful of the power of words. Words can make people feel strong. They can cause pain. They can heal.

Get paper. Cut out a big heart. Think of all the mean things that you've heard people say. Write them down on the heart. Each time you write something down, fold the paper. When you're done, unfold the paper. See the wrinkles. Try to rub the wrinkles out.

What did you learn? The wrinkles can't be taken away. In the same way, mean words can't be taken away. They're like the wrinkles. You can heal. But the pain will always be there.

Tip: Do an act of kindness. Do it for someone you know. Or do it for a stranger.

Some people are treated unfairly. They're treated unfairly because they're different. If you see someone being treated unfairly, show empathy. Let people know that you see them. Let them know that you're an **ally**. An ally is a friend. Here are some ways you can help:

- Say something. Address the person who is in pain. For example, say, "I saw that. Are you okay? Do you need to talk?" Make sure the person doesn't feel alone.
- Speak up. Address the person who caused the pain. For example, say, "I thought what you said was unfair. Imagine if someone said that to you. How would that make you feel?"

Tip: Smile. Be open to new friends.

CHAPTER SIX
Solve Problems

Conflict is a part of life. Conflicts are fights or problems. Everybody has conflicts. Most conflicts start with mistakes. Most people don't really mean to hurt each other. Try to turn conflicts into learning moments. Practice empathy. Learning how to resolve a conflict is an important life skill.

Understand the reason for conflicts. Think about your role in the conflict. Consider these questions:

- What happened?
- What were you feeling or thinking before the conflict?
- What were you feeling or thinking during the conflict?
- What were you feeling or thinking after the conflict?
- Who has been affected by the conflict? How?
- What could you have done better?

Tip: Describe your feelings using the weather. If you're worried and sad, you might say, "Dark clouds are in the sky. It's pouring rain."

Always try to see conflicts from the other person's view. Think about details you may have missed. Consider these questions:

- What is the person feeling? What makes you think that?
- Why did the person participate in the conflict?
- What were the **triggers**? Triggers are things that set off a certain behavior.

Meet with the person. Solve your conflicts together. Consider these questions:

- How did we hurt each other?
- What did we learn from talking to each other?
- How can we make things better?
- How can we make sure this doesn't happen again?

Tip: Create a peace table. This is where you can go to solve conflicts.

Fun Fact

Studies have shown the benefits of reading fiction. People who read more fiction have more empathy. They can see themselves in the stories. They relate to the characters. They get lost in stories. Their attitudes and ideas change. So, reading fiction makes us better people! The most popular fiction today is the Harry Potter series. The series has earned many world records. J. K. Rowling is the author of the Harry Potter books. She holds a world record for selling a fiction book the fastest within 24 hours. On July 21, 2007, *Harry Potter and the Deathly Hallows* went on sale. The book sold 8.3 million copies in 24 hours. About 345,833 books were sold each hour. Rowling holds another record. She's the highest-paid children's book author. She's the first billion-dollar author. She's 1 of only 5 women who are self-made billionaires.

HOST YOUR OWN MINDFULNESS EVENT!

Feeling sad? Feeling happy? Feeling a lot of emotions? This might be the best time to host your own mindfulness event! Host a "Show Empathy" Party!

STEP ONE: Figure out where you can host your party. You'll need space to spread out.

STEP TWO: Make invitations—and get creative! Ask a friend to help you. Send out the invitations.

STEP THREE: Plan your activities and get supplies.

Shoe Game!

- Everyone sits in a circle.
- Each person takes off a shoe. Put the shoes in the middle of the circle.
- Count to 3. Tell everyone to grab a shoe that is not their own.
- Have each person try to find the shoe's owner. The people will now be partners. You might have more than one partner!
- Shoe partners will learn what it's like to walk in the other person's shoes. Take turns interviewing each other. Ask questions that will help you learn more about each other.
- After 10 minutes, come back as a group. Have each person share something they learned about their partner. After they shared, they can return the shoe.

Emotions Charades!

- Hand each person 5 pieces of paper. Have each person write down 5 emotions. Write 1 emotion per paper.
- Fold the papers. Put them in a jar.
- Have each person pull out a paper from the jar. Each person needs to act out the emotion. They can use body movements and words.
- Ask others to guess the emotion. Then, talk about the emotion. Ask these questions: When do you feel this emotion? Does this emotion make you feel good or bad? How can we make ourselves feel better?

Worries Connections!

- Give everyone an index card. Have everyone write something that worries them. Tell them not to write their names.
- Shuffle the cards.
- Give out the cards.
- Sit in a circle. Have each person read the card. Have them share how they can relate to the card.
- Tell everyone they shouldn't feel alone in their worries. Say, "We all have fears and worries." Ask, "How can we help each other?"

GLOSSARY

affirm (uh-FURM) to support or validate

ally (AL-eye) a friend or supporter

biases (BYE-uhs-iz) having preferences for ideas that may prevent you from giving an equal chance to other ideas

conflict (KAHN-flikt) fight, problem, or argument

current (KUR-uhnt) happening right now

emotions (ih-MOH-shuhnz) feelings

empathy (EM-puh-thee) feeling another person's emotions

grudges (GRUHJ-iz) bad feelings of resentment brought on when someone wrongs you

interrupt (in-tuh-RUHPT) to cut in before one's turn

mindful (MINDE-ful) focusing one's awareness on the present moment to center the mind, body, and soul

points of view (POINTS UHV VYOO) perspectives or specific ways of seeing things based on position

role-playing (ROHL-play-ing) acting out the part of a character

shelter (SHEL-tur) a place that offers protection from bad weather or danger, such as a home

small talk (SMAWL TAWK) polite chatter about unimportant things like weather

triggers (TRIG-urz) things that set off a certain behavior

INDEX

About the Author

Dr. Virginia Loh-Hagan is an author, university professor, and former classroom teacher. She cries every time she watches a movie with dogs. She lives in San Diego with her very tall husband and very naughty dogs.